After Dinner

More Jokes and Funny Stories for Speechmakers

Compiled by Hugh Morrison

Montpelier Publishing

London

2015

ISBN-13: 978-1511617239

ISBN-10: 1511617233

Published by Montpelier Publishing, London.

Printed by Amazon Createspace.

Academics

An elderly Oxford don was asked by his wife why he got drunk so often at night in his study.

'When one is alone, the port does seem to come round so much more often,' explained the academic.

A prominent atheist academic was the guest of honour at an Oxford college dinner. Just before the meal commenced, the Dean leant over to him and explained that it was strict college tradition to say Grace before eating.

Since the chaplain was off sick, it was also college tradition that the duty should then fall to the principal speaker. Not wishing to be rude, but acutely aware of his reputation, the academic rose to his feet and solemnly declared:

'There being no clergyman present, let us thank God.'

Two elderly classicists, one from Oxford and the other from Cambridge met for dinner.

'What type of wine would you like?' asked the Oxfordian.

'Hock,' replied the Cambridge man.

'What was that? Asked the other, who was a little deaf.

'I said Hock. As in, *hic, haec, hoc.*'

Half an hour later the dinner had begun but no wine had been served.

'I thought I asked for hock,' said the Cantabrian.

'You did indeed,' said the Oxfordian, 'but you afterwards declined it.'

A mathematician was asked how to divide four pints of beer between himself and his two colleagues using strict logic only.

He pushed two of the pint glasses across the table to the two men.

'Here's two for you two.'

Then he pushed the other two pints to his side of the table and said 'and here's two for me, too.'

In Georgian Oxford a scholar put his horse into a field belonging to Merton College, after which the Master sent him a message, that if he continued to keep his horse there, he would cut off his tail. The scholar told the messenger, 'go tell your master, if he cuts off my horse's tail, I will cut off his ears.' This being delivered to the Master, he in a passion sent for the scholar, who appeared before him. He said sternly, 'How now, Sir, what mean you by that menace you sent me?' 'Sir,' said the youth, 'I menaced you not; I only said, if you cut off my horse's tail, I would cut off his ears'

Actors

A story is told by a good-humoured celebrity that when a man once stood before him and his friend at the theatre, completely shutting out all view of the stage, instead of asking him to sit down, or in any way giving offence, he simply said, 'I beg your pardon, sir; but when you see or hear anything particularly interesting on the stage, will you please let us know, as we are entirely dependent on your kindness?'

'I've seen you on stage, haven't I?'

'Quite possibly my dear fellow. I do appear, on and off. How do you like me?'

'Off.'

A prominent actor was continually disturbed in his performance by the ringing of a mobile phone somewhere in the auditorium. To add insult to injury, the ring tone was a particularly annoying pop tune.

Finally, the actor stepped forward and solemnly announced:

'Ladies and gentlemen, I regret that if this play is not stopped immediately, the musical recital cannot continue.'

The guilty party took the hint, and the phone was switched off to applause.

A jobbing actor finally got his first leading role in a major film. In one scene he had to jump off a high diving board in to a swimming pool. He climbed to the top of the board, looked down and promptly climbed down again.

`What's the matter?' asked the director.

'I can't jump from that board!' said the actor. `Do you know there's only one foot of water in that pool?'

'Of course,' said the director. `We don't want you to drown, you know.'

A man went to the doctor with a hideous skin infection on his arm.

The doctor looked at it in horror.

'How on earth did you get this?' he asked.

'Well doctor,' said the man. 'It's like this. I work in the circus, but before the elephants go on stage, I have to stick my arm up their back passages to clean them out in case they make a mess on the floor.'

The doctor recoiled in disgust.

'You've obviously caught this infection from it,' he said. 'Can't you find another job?'

'What!?' exclaimed the man. 'And give up show business?'

The late Sir John Gielgud was once accosted by a persistent fan outside the theatre.

'What's going on, Sir John?' asked the fan.

The actor replied politely as he dodged the fan: 'I am. Please excuse me.'

Africa

Two explorers were lost in a remote part of the jungle when they came across a leopard. The animal snarled and began to approach them with the clear intention of eating them.

'We're out of ammunition, we'll have to run for it!' whispered Carstairs.

'My good man – you don't seriously expect you can outrun a leopard?' replied Carruthers.

'My dear chap,' explained Carstairs, 'I don't have to outrun him. I only have to outrun *you*. '

A Victorian railway engineer in Africa was trying to explain the advantages of the new railway line to a local tribe, who were reluctant to have the line cross their land.

'How long does it take you to drive your cattle to market?' asked the engineer of the village chief.

'Three days,' replied the Chief.

'Well then,' said the engineer, 'when the line is built, you can take your animals to market on the train and be there and back in one day.'

'That is very well, but what shall we do with the other two days?' replied the chief.

Alcohol

Wife (to drunken husband). What do you mean by coming home at three o'clock in the morning?

Husband: It's only one o'clock. I'll swear to it that I heard the church clock strike one while I was lying in the gutter.

Wife: How can you be so sure?

Husband: I heard it at least three times!

McPherson: There's a terrible drunkard over in that field. He's drinkin' oot o' two bottles at once!

McNab: Dinnae be daft. He's looking oot of a pair o' binoculars!

A drunk staggered out of a pub into the car park. He stopped in front of the first car he came to, touched the roof and said 'Not this one.' He swayed over to the next car, touched the roof for a few seconds and said again, 'not this one.' As he weaved his way to the next car, a customer who was watching him asked 'How do you expect to find your car just by touching the roof?'

The drunk replied 'Cos mine's the one with the big blue light on top.'

An English tourist was on holiday in Belgium, that great beer making country, when he was intrigued by a sign above a shop which read 'Beer Baths, 10 Euros'. He went in an asked the attendant what a beer bath was.

'This monsieur, is a healthy bath for the skin using the Belgian beer. The little bubbles, they improve the skin.'

The attendant showed the Englishman the bath full of beer, with a number of corpulent Belgian men scrubbing themselves in it.

'What happens when the customer has finished bathing in the beer?' asked the man.

'We have a discounted entry, for people to wash in the same beer, for only two euros.'

'And what do you do with the beer after that?'

'After that, monsieur, we put it into barrels and sell it.'

'Good Lord!' exclaimed the Englishman. 'You don't mean to tell me that Belgians drink that stuff?'

'Certainly not, monsieur,' replied the Belgian. 'We send it to English pubs to be sold as lager.'

Magistrate (to man arrested for being drunk and disorderly on a train): Have you anything to say in your defence?

Defendant: Yes sir. I got drunk because of the group I was with on the train.

Magistrate: And what was this group?

Defendant: Alcoholics Anonymous, sir.

Magistrate: I should have thought that was the best company you could have wished for.

Defendant: Not really sir. I had to drink my bottle of whisky all by myself.

Priest: Look here Seamus, I thought you'd cut down on drinking?

Seamus: Tis true I have, father. I've only had twelve drinks since last month.

Priest: Then how is it you're drunk as a lord today?'

Seamus: I had 'em all this mornin'!

Army

When the Territorial Army was set up in the nineteenth century, a number of volunteers sent a delegation to the colonel in chief to state that they were willing to join, but were not willing to leave the country.

'Except in the case of an actual invasion, I suppose,' replied the colonel.

In the Great War, an Irish soldier called out to his officer across no man's land:

'Sor, I've taken a prisoner.'

'Bring him along then man; bring him along!'

'He won't come sor.'

'Then come yourself.'

'He won't let me sor.'

Barbers

A balding man complained to his barber that his hair was falling out.

'Can't you give me anything to keep it in?' asked the man.

'A cardboard box?' suggested the barber.

Many years ago a minister was being shaved by a barber who was the worse for drink. After the man had cut him three times, the minister proclaimed:

'The drink has a terrible effect, has it not?'

'Indeed sir,' said the barber with a wink. 'It makes the skin mair tender.'

A hippy went to the barbers.

'Haven't I seen you before?' asked the hippy.

'I don't think so sir,' said the barber. 'I've only worked here six months.'

Birthdays

'What's your husband getting for his fortieth birthday?'

'Bald and fat.'

A Scottish Birthday Greeting:

Forget about the past, you can't change it.

Forget about the future, you can't predict it.

Forget about the present, I didn't get you one.

Wife: (to henpecked husband): No need to wash the dishes tonight, dear. After all, it's your birthday.

Husband: Thank you dear.

Wife: Yes, you can leave them until tomorrow.

It's my wife's birthday tomorrow. Last week I asked her what she wanted as a present. 'Oh, I don't know,' she said. 'Just give me something with lots of diamonds. That's why I'm giving her a pack of playing cards.

A man's wife's birthday and her father's birthday fell on the same day. He bought a bottle of perfume for his wife, and wrote a note saying 'Use this on yourself and think of me.' He bought his father in law a shotgun, and wrote a note saying 'Here's something for next time you go hunting. I hope you catch something interesting.' The presents were duly delivered; the perfume to his wife and the shotgun to his father in law. Unfortunately he mixed the notes up.

Little Johnny: Mummy, do you know what I'm going to give you for your birthday?

Mom: No, dear, what?

Little Johnny: A nice teapot.

Mom: But I've got a nice teapot.

Little Johnny: No you haven't. I've just dropped it.

Wife: Why didn't you give me anything for my birthday?

Husband: You told me to surprise you!

'I'm 96 tomorrow, vicar, and I haven't an enemy in the world.'

'That is wonderful. You must truly have a forgiving nature.'

'No, I've just outlived them all!'

A Jewish mother gave her son two ties for his birthday; one red, one blue. The next time the son visited, he wore one of the ties to show his appreciation. When the lady opened her door she looked her son up and down scornfully and said 'So the red tie wasn't good enough for you?'

Business

'When did you start working here?'

'When the boss told me he'd sack me if I didn't.'

The pretty young secretary was talking to her boss. 'I have some good news and some bad news.'

'What's the good news?' asked the boss.

'You're not sterile.'

The eminent financier was discoursing. 'The true secret of success,' he said, 'is to find out what the people want.'

'And the next thing,' someone suggested, 'is to give it to them.'

The financier shook his head contemptuously. 'No — to corner the market.'

A business guru told me 'always follow your dreams.' So I went back to bed.

'We pay great attention to hygiene in this office,' said the manager as he showed the interviewee round the building. 'Did you wipe your feet on the doormat as you came in?' 'Oh yes sir,' said the hopeful visitor. 'We also pay great attention to honesty,' said the manager. 'The doormat was removed for cleaning this morning.'

In the first class section of a transatlantic jet, a businessman became increasingly annoyed by the man next to him who kept falling asleep and snoring loudly.

Recognising the man as the head of a well known soft drinks company known for its secret ingredient, the businessman said to him when he woke up, 'pardon me sir, but I couldn't help overhearing you talking in your sleep. Something about a "secret formula"?'

The man was too worried to go back to sleep and his neighbour got a good night's rest.

Charity

A charity collector for African famine relief knocked on the door of a big mansion and asked for a donation.

'No, sorry,' came the reply from the man who lived there.

'Come now,' said the collector. 'With this big house, surely you have some money to spare?'

'Yes I've got a big house,' said the man. 'But did you also know I have two children with university bills to pay?'

'Er...no,' replied the collector.

'And a mother in law who's old and bedridden and needs round the clock care?'

'Er...no,' replied the collector again, beginning to feel a little embarrassed. 'I'm very sorry to have troubled you, sir.'

The man continued. 'And a very sick wife who needs an expensive life saving operation?'

As the collector shamefully left the doorstep, the man shouted after him:

'And if I don't give a penny to any of them, why should I care about Africa?!'

Headline in a parish magazine: 'I upped my planned giving – up yours!'

McNab was passing through a small highland town and knocked on the door of the manse.

'Minister, ye did me a favour ten years ago,' said McNab, 'and I have nivver forgotten it.'

'Ah,' replied the clergyman with a holy expression on his face, 'as the good book says, "there is more joy in heaven over one sinner that repenteth" – you've come back to repay me?'

'Not exactly,' replied McNab. 'I've just got into toon and need another favour, and I thought of you right away.'

A tramp accosted a kind-hearted woman on Westminster Bridge and she gave him a pound.

The beggar thanked her profusely. 'Things was looking pretty bad until you came along. I'd even thought about the last resort.'

'You don't mean...suicide?' gasped the woman, looking down at the icy waters of the Thames below.

'No, finding a job,' replied the tramp.

Louis XI, in his youth, used to visit a peasant, whose garden produced excellent fruit. When he ascended the throne, his friend presented him a turnip of extraordinary size. The king smiled, and remembering his past pleasures, ordered a thousand crowns to the peasant. The lord of the village hearing of this liberality, thus argued with himself: 'If this fellow get a thousand crowns for his turnip, I have only to present a capital horse to the munificent monarch, and my fortune is made.'

Accordingly he carried to court a beautiful horse, and requested his majesty's acceptance of it. Louis highly praised the steed, and the donor's expectation was raised to the highest, when the king called out, 'Bring me my turnip!' and presenting it to the squire, added, 'This turnip cost me a thousand crowns, and I give it you for your horse.'

Children

Little Johnny was at a toy shop. He picked up a car, went up to the counter and handed over some play money to the assistant.

'This isn't real money, you know,' said the man.

'So what,' replied Little Johnny. This isn't a real car either.'

Little Johnny was looking through old photos in the family album. 'Mummy, who's this handsome young man next to you?'

'That's your father.'

'Then who's that bald old man who lives with us?'

Father (about to spank his naughty son): Now then my boy, this will hurt me more than it will hurt you.

Son: Then why don't you let me spank you instead?

Mother: Little Johnny, daddy and I are going to have a new baby.

Little Johnny: Why? Don't you like the old one anymore?

Mother: Little Johnny, what are you doing?

Little Johnny: I'm writing a letter.

Mother: To whom?

Little Johnny: Myself.

Mother: What does it say?

Little Johnny: I don't know. I haven't received it yet.

Little Johnny: Mummy, can I go swimming at the beach?

Mother: No dear, there are very dangerous currents.

Little Johnny: But daddy swims there.

Mother: Yes dear. But he has life insurance.

Mother: Johnny, I forbid you to go to Jimmy's house. He's very rude.

Little Johnny: That's alright mother. I'm not rude, so can Jimmy come here instead?

Christenings

'What is the name of this boy,' asked the clergyman as his mother passed the baby to him.

'It's a girl,' said the mother. 'Let go of my finger!'

From church magazine: 'Because of repair work by the west door, for the next few weeks we are going to christen babies at the other end. '

Little Johnny was at a christening and was very interested in the baby boy.

'Can I have a little brother, mummy?' he whispered.

No dear,' replied his mother. 'Your father doesn't want one.'

'Can't we surprise him?'

Clergy

A story has been told of a nineteenth-century wag who gained access to the Clarendon printing office in Oxford, when a new edition of the prayer book was ready for the press. In that part of the 'form' already set up which contained the marriage service, he substituted the letter k for the letter v in the word live; and thus the vow 'to love, honour, comfort, etc., so long as you both shall live,' was made to read 'so long as you both shall like!'

A journalist was interviewing people for an article on modern attitudes to marriage. He phoned the local vicar. 'What value does the church place on marriage these days?' asked the reporter. There was a pause as the vicar considered the question, then he replied:

'About £300, including the organist.'

A Sunday school teacher was telling the story of the Good Samaritan. Afterwards she asked the children 'Why did the priest and the Levite pass by on the other side?'

Little Johnny put up his hand. 'Because the man had been robbed already?'

'In order to streamline the confession process,' announced a young Catholic priest very concerned with order and method, 'I am changing the way I hear confession this week. On Mondays, I will hear confession from the drunkards, on Tuesday from the fornicators, on Wednesday from the adulterers on Thursday the thieves, on Friday the liars and on Saturday the gluttons.'

Nobody turned up for confession that week.

A young man wanted to marry a Catholic girl but wasn't sure if the priest would allow it since he was not a Catholic himself.

'What is your religion?' asked the priest of the young man.

'I'm an agnostic,' he replied.

'What do you mean by that, exactly?' asked the priest.

'It means to not be sure of anything,' said the man.

'In that case, how do you know you're an agnostic?' replied the priest.

'The good news is, there is enough money to pay for the restoration of the church roof,' said the vicar during morning service. As the congregation sighed with relief, he continued, 'the bad news is it's still in your pockets.'

A good looking priest found the young ladies in the church rather too interested in him. At last it became so embarrassing that he left. Not long afterwards he met the priest who had succeeded him.

'Well,' he asked, 'how do you get on with the ladies?'

'Oh, very well indeed,' said the other. 'There is safety in numbers, you know.'

'Ah!' was the instant reply. 'I only found it in Exodus.'

A beggar approached a clergyman and asked for assistance.

'Please help a poor preacher, sir.'

The clergyman, suspicious that it might be a ruse to take advantage of his good nature, replied 'If you're a preacher, tell me what book follows the gospel of St John in the Bible.'

'That I can't,' said the beggar.

'I thought you said you were a poor preacher,' said the clergyman.

'I am that sir, and such a poor one that I've never read the Bible.'

A story is told of nineteenth century preacher Lorenzo Dow, who was arrested and imprisoned for slander after mentioning a prominent wealthy man in one of his sermons.

Following his release from jail, he began his sermon with the text 'There was a rich man who died and went to....' then he paused, and continued, 'but I will not say where he went, in case any of his relations are in this congregation and wish to sue me for defamation of character.'

A vicar told his congregation, 'Next week I plan to preach about the sin of lying. To help you understand my sermon, I want you all to read St Mark chapter 17.'

The following Sunday, as he prepared to deliver his sermon, the minister asked for a show of hands. He asked how many had read St Mark chapter 17. Every hand went up. The vicar smiled and said, 'The gospel of St Mark has only sixteen chapters. I will now proceed with my sermon on the sin of lying.'

A new vicar, who was very lazy, stepped up into his new church's pulpit for the first time.

'Do you know what I am going to say to you?' he asked.

'No,' responded the congregation.

'Well then, there is no use speaking to you,' said the clergyman, and stepped down.

The following Sunday, he asked again. 'Do you know what I am going to say to you?'

'We know,' replied the congregation.

'If you know, then why should I bother telling you?' replied the vicar, and stepped down.

The next Sunday he asked again. 'Do you know what I am going to say to you?'

The congregation were getting fed up and decided on a different tactic. 'Some of us do, and some of us don't,' they replied.

'Well,' said the vicar, 'those of you who know, tell those of you who don't,' and stepped down.

In the early days of Queen Victoria's reign, the Bishop of Oxford sent round to the churchwardens in his diocese a list of inquiries, among which was the question: 'Does your officiating clergyman preach the gospel, and is his conversation and carriage consistent therewith?' The churchwarden near Wallingford replied: 'He preaches the gospel, but cannot afford to keep a carriage.'

Clubs

A member of a club in London posted a notice on the board demanding that the nobleman who stole his umbrella at once return it. When a fellow member asked how he knew that the culprit was a noblemen he replied, 'Sir, the rules of this club state that it is for noblemen and gentlemen. And no gentleman would have taken my umbrella.'

At an exclusive country club three men walked past a woman sunbathing on the lawn, completely naked except for a copy of the Times covering her face from the glare.

'Good Lord, I think that's my wife!' exclaimed the first man, looking down at the woman's body.

'I can assure you it's not,' said the second, looking down as well.

The third man scrutinised the woman's body for some time and then said:

'All I know is she's not one of the ladies in this club.'

Cricket

A poor, badly equipped church cricket team was scheduled a match against a much more successful team from a wealthier parish. Desperate to improve the reputation of his parish, the vicar gave £500 to the team's captain.

'This is for new pads, bats, gloves – in fact anything that will help you win the match.'

The church team was victorious and the vicar went to the pavilion to congratulate the players.

When he saw the team up close, he realised they were still using their old equipment.

'What happened to the five hundred pounds I gave you?' he asked.

'Well vicar,' explained the captain, 'you said it was for anything that would help us win the match. So we gave it to the umpire.'

'Why are you so depressed?'

'My doctor says I can't play cricket anymore.'

'Really? I didn't think he'd ever seen you play.'

'Do you ever have a hard job explaining the game to your wife?' asked one cricket team member of another.

'I did last week,' came the reply. 'She found out I wasn't there.'

The two rival cricketers were talking.

'The local team wants me to play for them very badly.'

'Well, you're just the man for the job.'

Doctors

A private surgeon was about to perform a serious operation on a nervous patient.

'Now don't worry old chap,' said the surgeon. 'I've performed hundreds of operations like this one.'

'You must be a very rich man then,' said the patient. 'Not really,' replied the surgeon. 'I only get paid by the patients who survive.'

Doctor: Don't you know that smoking shortens your life?

Patient: I'm not so sure. My father smokes 60 a day, and he's eighty years old this year.

Doctor: Well if he'd never smoked he might have been ninety by now!

A miser was convinced he needed medical help from top private doctors, but was too mean to pay for it. One day he was seated next to a Harley Street doctor at a dinner party. He contrived to introduce the matter of his illness into the conversation, dropping lots of hints. After none of these worked he came straight out and asked the wearied doctor what he should take for it.

'Professional advice,' came the reply.

Not to be put off so easily, the miser persisted.

'But what would you take for it?' the miser asked.

'A fee,' said the doctor.

An obese man was advised by his doctor that he should regularly go for a walk on an empty stomach.

'Yes, but whose stomach should I walk on?' replied the confused patient.

Paddy was seeing a psychiatrist. The doctor showed him a book of Rorschach inkblots.

'What does this remind you of?' said the doctor.

'Sex,' said Paddy without hesitation.

The doctor flipped the page. 'And this one?'

'Sex,' replied Paddy again.

Turning to another page, the doctor asked again.

'What about this one.' 'Sex.'

This went on for some time until the doctor had gone through several books of inkblots.

'You appear to have an obsession with sex,' said the doctor, finally.

'Huh!' said Paddy in disgust. 'You're the one with all the dirty books.'

A prison doctor was discussing a prisoner's test results.

'I've got some good news and some bad news, prisoner 15447,' said the doctor.

'What's the good news?'

'You'll be out of here in a week.'

Prisoner 15447 was amazed. 'But doc, I'm supposed to be here for the rest of my life!'

'Ah,' said the doctor awkwardly. 'That brings me on to the bad news...'

'Do you think I shall live until I'm ninety, doctor?'

'How old are you now?'

'Forty.'

'Do you drink, smoke, take drugs, or go with loose women?'

'Certainly not. I've no vices of any kind.'

'Well, what do you want to live another fifty years for?'

Sir Samuel Garth, physician to George I, was a member of the infamous Kit-Kat Club. Coming to the club one night, he said he must soon be gone, having many patients to attend; but some good wine was produced, and he forgot them. The author Sir Richard Steele was one of the party, and reminded him of the visits he had to pay. Garth pulled out his list, which amounted to fifteen, and said, 'It's no great matter whether I see them tonight or not; for nine of them, have such bad constitutions that all the physicians in the world can't save them ; and the other six have such good constitutions that all the physicians in the world can't kill them.'

In Victorian London a physician treated a man who had a reputation as being very careful with his money.

After the man had miraculously recovered, his wife visited the doctor and presented him with a beautiful embroidered purse.

'Please accept this as a token of my appreciation. It is handmade. '

The doctor sighed as he looked at the purse.

'It's very pretty, ma'am, but presents only maintain friendship. They don't maintain families.'

'What is your fee?' asked the wife.

'Five guineas,' replied the doctor.

The woman opened the purse and removed ten guineas. She put back five, and gave it to the doctor.

Doctor: I can't find any reason for your headaches. Perhaps it's because of excessive drinking?

Mc Tavish: Alright then doc, I'll come back later when ye've sobered up a bit!

A member of the faculty in a London medical college was appointed an honorary physician to the Queen. He proudly wrote a notice on the blackboard in his classroom:

'Professor Jennings informs his students that he has been appointed honorary physician to Her Majesty Queen Elizabeth the Second.'

When he returned to the class-room in the afternoon he found written below his notice this line:

'God save the Queen.'

The henpecked husband of a hypochondriac wife was despatched to the chemist's shop with a prescription.

Knowing the lady well, the pharmacist gave the medicine to the man and said 'Run back home as fast as you can. Don't stop for anything.'

'Good heavens,' replied the husband. 'Is it as bad as all that?'

'Certainly,' said the chemist. 'If you don't, she's likely to be better by the time you get back and you'll have wasted your money.'

A case was being heard where a private doctor had been accused of overcharging a patient. A nurse was asked whether she thought the doctor did not make several visits after the patient was out of danger. 'No,' replied the nurse. 'I considered the patient in danger as long as the doctor continued his visits.'

A man was hit by a car and lay in the road moaning in pain. The driver jumped out and said 'You're lucky. We're in front of a doctor's surgery.' 'Yes,' groaned the man. 'Except I'm the doctor.'

Divorce

Smith took his wife to a restaurant. He noticed a drunk man at the bar looking the worse for wear.

He whispered to his wife: 'Who's that man? I know him from somewhere.'

His wife sniffed. 'That's Joan's ex-husband. He started drinking when he left her last year and he hasn't been sober since.'

'Good Lord!' exclaimed Smith. 'I'd never have thought a fellow could celebrate that long!'

Wife: I have some good news and some bad news. First, I'm leaving you.

Husband: So what's the bad news?

'I hear you've just got divorced. How did your wife take it?'

'In cash.'

Judge (to witness): Were you aware of the quarrel between the couple?

Witness: Yes, it started three years ago.

Judge: As long ago as that?

Witness: Certainly. I was one of the guests at their wedding.

Irishmen

A stuck-up English landowner liked to boast to his friends of the rustic characters on his estate in Ireland, and what ridiculously far-fetched stories they liked to tell him.

During a shooting party he called out to one of the beaters.

'Here, you, Paddy, or Seamus or whatever your name is, I'll give you a glass of whiskey if you can tell me the biggest lie you know!'

'Begorrah sir,' replied the man. 'You're a true gentleman!'

After lunch Paddy returned to work drunk, and the foreman sent him home with a stern warning that he'd be fired if it happened again.

The next morning, Paddy arrived for work drunk.

'Didn't I tell you I'd fire you if had another drinking binge?' asked the foreman angrily.

'Sure an' I wasn't on another drinking binge!' objected Paddy. 'I'm still on the same one!'

Sign over a ford in County Kerry: 'When the water is over this sign the road is impassable.'

An old Irish republican was on his deathbed, making his final confession to the priest.

'O'Toole,' warned the priest, 'you must forgive even your worst enemies now.'

'You don't mean those devilish protestant sadists of Englishmen, surely, father?'

'I do indeed, my son,' replied the priest. 'You must forgive them all.'

'Well then, and I forgive them,' said O'Toole.

Then he turned to his son beside him.

'But my everlasting curse be upon you if *you* start forgiving them,' he said.

Priest: 'I see the devil in every bottle of whiskey'.

Paddy: 'There's never a truer reflection I'm sure, father!

Seamus burst into the priest's house one morning.

'Come quickly father, for Paddy's fallen into a bog and can't get out.'

'Sure and it can't be so bad as to require the last rites, can it now?' replied the clergyman.

'He's up to his ankles!' cried Seamus.

'Only up to his ankles? Then what do you need me for?' asked the priest, somewhat annoyed.

'He fell in head first!'

'How's business, Paddy?', asked one Dublin shopkeeper of another.

'Not so bad Seamus, some days we make nothin' at all, but other days we make twice as much!'

Seamus: I've finally managed to give up drinking.

Paddy: Let's have a drink on that!

Paddy moved to England. The Queen's Jubilee was coming up and thought he'd show loyalty to his new country by buying a Union Flag to hang from his window. 'Give me a British flag,' he asked a shopkeeper. 'But since I'm Irish,' he continued, 'You'd better give me one in green.' 'I'm sorry sir,' said the shopkeeper. 'The British flag only comes in red, white and blue.'

Paddy thought for a moment. 'Alright then, I'll take a red one,' he replied.

A silver-tongued Irishman was asked by two sisters to guess which one of them was younger.

'Sure and you both look younger than the other,' replied the charmer.

Journalists

A journalist was interviewing a man who had been rescued from drowning after falling into the canal in a drunken stupor.

Hoping for a good 'human interest' story, the reporter asked 'And did your life flash before your eyes?'

'I wouldn't know,' replied the man. 'I had them shut the whole time.'

A newspaper seller on a street corner was shouting 'Big scam, 38 victims!' A man, interested to find out more, bought a paper. The seller started shouting again. 'Big scam, 39 victims!'

Lawyers

Barrister: You seem to be very intelligent for a woman in your profession.

Witness: If I wasn't under oath, I'd return the compliment.

After a severe cross-examination, the counsel for the prosecution paused, and then putting on a look of severity, and an ominous shake of the head, exclaimed to the witness:

'I put it to you, that an effort has been made to induce you to tell a different story.'

'A different story from what I've told, sir?'

'That is what I mean.'

'Yes sir; several people have tried to get me to tell a different story from what I have told, but they couldn't.'

'I wish to know who those persons are.'

'Well, I think you've tried about as hard as any of them.'

Lawyer (to businessman): What did the customer say when you asked for payment?

Businessman: He told me to go to the devil.

Lawyer: And what did you do next?

Businessman: I came to you.

Magistrate (to female witness): Are you a friend of the prisoner?

Witness: No, I'm his wife.

Barrister (to female witness): And did your husband hit you between the two aforementioned occurrences?

Witness: No, just between the eyes.

Tramp: (to man about to enter divorce court) 'Spare a penny before you go in, guv'nor?'

Man: 'What for?'

Tramp: 'Chances are you won't have one when you come out.'

Magistrate (to prisoner): What brought you here?

Prisoner: A police van, sir.

Magistrate: And I suppose disorderly conduct has nothing to do with it?

Prisoner: Yes sir, the police were very rough with me.

Married life

Wife (to husband): Why do you keep looking at our marriage certificate?

Husband: I want to see if there's a get-out clause.

Husband: Darling, I've bought you a silver wedding present.

Wife: What is it?

Husband: A trip to Africa.

Wife: That's amazing. What will you do for our golden wedding?

Husband: I'll come and get you.

Ella: Who's your favourite writer?

Bella: My husband.

Ella: What does he write?

Bella: Cheques.

'You've only yourself to please,' said the married man to the bachelor.

'True,' replied the bachelor, 'but you've no idea how hard that is.'

The newly married couple arrived in their new home. The husband decided he would lay down some rules. 'My dear,' he said to his wife, 'I want you to understand that I am the master of this house.

'When I come home from work, you will cook a meal for me. Then you will fill a bath for me.

'After that, you will polish my shoes. Finally, I'm going to get undressed. Who do you think is going to do that for me?'

'The undertaker,' replied his wife.

Husband: Darling that was an excellent meal. Where did you get the recipe?

Wife: From an Agatha Christie book.

Matches are made in heaven. On earth, they're usually just sold.

'My wife's not speaking to me.'

'Why's that?'

'I've no idea. The other night she looked at me all strangely and said "Do what you want with me!"'

'So I sent her off to her mother's for a few days.'

A hotel receptionist received a phone call from a man in a room on the top floor. 'You've got to help me,' said the man. 'I've just had an argument with my wife and she's threatening to throw herself out of the window.'

'I'd better call the police,' said the receptionist.

'No,' said the man. 'Call a maintenance man. The window won't open.'

The newly married pair quarrelled seriously, so that the wife in a passion finally declared:

'I'm going home to my mother!'

The husband maintained his calm in the face of this calamity, and drew out his wallet.

'Here,' he said, counting out some notes, 'is the money for your train fare.'

The wife took it, and counted it as well. Then she faced her husband scornfully:

'That isn't enough for a return ticket.'

What do you call a man who has lost his mind? A widower.

Take warning from the unfortunate young man who, every time he met the father of his wife, complained to him of the bad temper of his daughter. At last the old gentleman, weary of the grumbling of his son-in-law, exclaimed: 'You're damned right, she's rude and impertinent; and if I hear any more complaints about her, I will disinherit her.'

'See here,' said a fault-finding husband, 'we must have things arranged in this house so that we shall know where everything is kept.' 'With all my heart,' sweetly answered his wife, 'and let's begin with your late hours, my love. I should very much like to know where they are kept.'

A young couple that had received many valuable wedding presents started life in their new home. One morning they received in the post two tickets for a popular show in the city, with a single line:

'Guess who sent them.'

The pair had much amusement in trying to identify the donor, but failed in the effort. They duly attended the theatre, and had a delightful time. On their return home late at night, still trying to guess the identity of the unknown host, they found the house stripped of every article of value. And on the bare table in the dining-room was a piece of paper on which was written in the same handwriting as the enclosure with the tickets:

'Now you know!'

Husband: Darling, have you ever looked at a man and wished you were single again?

Wife: Yes dear. Every morning when I wake up.

'My dear,' said an affectionate wife, 'what shall we have for dinner to-day?'

'One of your smiles,' replied the husband. 'I can dine on that every day.'

'But I can't,' replied the wife.

'Then take this,' and he gave her a kiss and went off to work.

He returned to dinner.

'This is excellent steak,' he said. 'What did you pay for it?'

'Why, just what you gave me this morning,' replied the wife.

Fat husband: Where are my trousers? I told you to have them let out.

Wife: I did. The man next door's agreed to wear them until you lose weight.

'I curse the day we were married!' said a wife to her husband.

'But my dear,' replied the man, 'that was the only happy day we've had!'

An old Yorkshireman said to his wife 'the whole world's queer save thee and me...and sometimes I think thee's a bit queer too!'

Money

Jones was in financial difficulties and visited his solicitor to discuss bankruptcy.

'My fee will be £500 an hour,' said the lawyer.

'I'm here to solve my financial problems, not yours,' said Jones.

Did you hear about the man who swallowed a forged pound coin?

He was prosecuted for passing counterfeit money.

Mother: Johnny, your grandmother has just given you a pound for your money box. What do you say?

Little Johnny: Is that all?

A wealthy heiress announced her engagement to her father. The old man sighed. 'Does he have any money?' 'You men are all the same,' said the girl, angrily. 'He asked me exactly the same question about you before he proposed!'

A spendthrift was making fun of a miser, and pointed to his rather shabby coat.

'I see you still have your grandfather's coat,' he said, mockingly.

'Yes,' replied the miser. 'And his lands, too.'

A mugger robbed a man of his watch and money. He begged the thief to let him have cash enough for the bus fare home, and the mugger said, 'There's honour among thieves. I'll let you have five pounds.' The man reported the incident to the police who organised a line up of suspects.

The man immediately identified the mugger and demanded his watch and money back. 'I've no idea what you're talking about' said the mugger. 'I thought you wanted to pay me back the five pounds you borrowed off me.'

'I see old Lord Moneybags has died.'

'What did he leave behind?'

'Everything.'

Money is like promises – easier made than kept.

An elderly man inherited a thousand pounds in cash from a friend. Not trusting banks, he decided to hide some in an old teapot on a shelf in the kitchen. Unbeknownst to him, his home help noticed him doing this, and being a dishonest type, stole the money. When the man went to retrieve the money, he found it was gone. He suspected the home help but had no evidence, so he discretely had a cctv camera installed.

When the home help was cleaning one day, the blind man casually remarked to him, 'I've had a spot of luck recently. I won two thousand pounds on a horse. But I'm not sure what to do with it. I don't really trust banks so I'm thinking of hiding it in the house instead. There's a good little place I know that I'm already using. What do you suggest?'

The home help advised him immediately that banks couldn't be trusted and advised hiding it in the place he was already using. When the old man was out of the room, the home help rushed to the teapot to put the thousand pounds back, in case he was found out. It was at that moment that the old man caught the whole incident on a newly installed cctv camera.

The following verses were said to be inscribed over the doorway of an eighteenth century insurance office:

'Come all you men who love your wives

Insure large sums on your precarious lives

Your widows may be rich when you are rotten

And live in happiness when you are quite forgotten'

An accountant visited the wealthy father of his girlfriend. 'Sir,' he said, 'I can't go on living unless I marry your daughter.' 'Don't talk such romantic nonsense,' warned the father. ' I'm not being romantic,' said the young man. 'I've just audited my accounts!'

Mothers-in-law

There was a hold up at the local bank and the robber kept several people hostage in the bank.

He asked a man 'Did you see me rob the bank?'

'Y-yes sir,' said the man, terrified.

The robber pulled out a gun and shot him.

The robber then approached a family. He asked the man, 'Did you see me rob the bank?'

'No, but my mother-in-law did,' replied the man.

Wife: I have some good news and some bad news. My mother is coming to visit us.

Husband: And what's the good news?

Mother-in-law: George, sometimes I get the impression you dislike me living with you so much you'd like to kill me.

Son-in-law: If I did that I'd go to hell when I died – and I don't intend to spend eternity with you as well!

What is the penalty for bigamy?

Two mothers-in-law.

Husband: I've just seen a man insulting your mother.

Wife: I hope you intervened?

Husband: I didn't bother. He was managing it perfectly well without me.

Mother-in -law: (on doorstep). I've come to visit.

Son-in-law: How long for?

Mother-in-law: As long as you want me.

Son-in-law: Will you have a cup of tea before you go?

Musicians

After morning service in the cathedral, where a remarkably fine anthem had been performed, the page turner observed to the organist, 'I think we performed very well to-day.' '*We* performed?' answered the organist haughtily. 'If I am not mistaken it was *I* that performed.'

Next Sunday, in the midst of a voluntary, the page turner stopped turning the pages of the music. The organist, enraged, whispered, 'Why don't you turn the page?'

The young man coolly replied 'I thought it was you that was performing.'

A recording session had to stop when an oboe player, who was constantly sucking on her reed to keep it moist during rests and between takes, inadvertently inhaled and swallowed it.

The conductor immediately dialled 999 and asked what he should do.

The operator told him, 'Use muted trumpet instead.'

How can you tell when a soprano is at your door?

She can't find the key and doesn't know when to come in.

How many baritones does it take to change a lightbulb?

None. They can't get up that high.

'Haven't I seen your face before?' a judge demanded, looking down at the defendant. 'You have, your honour,' the man answered hopefully. 'I gave your son violin lessons last winter.' 'Ah, yes,' recalled the judge. 'Twenty years.'

Philosophers

A philosophical drunkard was found lying in the middle of the road by two policemen.

'Are you a fool, or just an idiot?' asked one of the constables, as he and his companion each took one of the man's arms.

'I believe I am somewhere between the two,' replied the man.

A story is told of a London taxi driver who picked up the philosopher Bertrand Russell in his cab. 'I said "Bertie, Bertie",' related the driver to his friends afterwards, '"you've written the History of Western Philosophy. You know the meaning of life. What's it all about?" Twit didn't know.'

Sherlock Holmes and Doctor Watson went on a camping trip.

Holmes woke Watson in the middle of the night.

'Watson,' said Holmes, 'look up at the sky and tell me what you see.'

Watson thought for a minute.

'Astronomically, it tells me that there are millions of galaxies and potentially billions of planets. Astrologically, I observe that Saturn is in Leo. Horologically, I deduce that the time is approximately a quarter past three. Theologically, I can see that God is all powerful and that we are small and insignificant. Meteorologically, I suspect that we will have a beautiful day tomorrow. What does it tell you?'

'That someone has stolen our tent.'

A hypocritical man in Athens put a sign over his door saying 'Let nothing evil enter here.' The philosopher Diogenes is said to have added underneath 'Which door does the owner use?'

Politicians

In 1930s Dublin a politician was campaigning for election to the Dail. He doorstepped Paddy and asked if he could count on his vote.

'Sure and aren't you the feller that was wounded in the uprising of 1916?' asked Paddy.

'I am that, sir,' said the politician.

'And aren't you the feller that was imprisoned by the British, and beaten up by them divils?'

'I am that, sir.'

'And aren't you the feller that lost a leg in the war of Independence in '22?

'I am that sir.'

'Sure, well and I think you've done enough for your country already. I'll vote for the other feller!'

Close by the Houses of Parliament a robber stuck a pistol into the back of a man and said 'Give me your money!'

The man was outraged and replied 'You can't say that to me, I'm a Member of Parliament!'

'In that case,' said the robber, 'give me all my money.'

Richard Brinsley Sheridan, (1751-1816) MP for Stafford, was one day much annoyed by a fellow member of the House of Commons, who kept shouting out every few minutes, 'Hear! hear!'

During the debate he took occasion to describe a political contemporary that wished to play the rogue, but had only sense enough to act the fool. 'Where,' he exclaimed, with great emphasis, 'where shall we find a more foolish knave or a more knavish fool than he?'

'Hear! hear!' was shouted by the troublesome member. Sheridan turned round, and, thanking him for the prompt information, sat down amid a general roar of laughter.

An American politician objected in Congress that the government of the United States did not abide by Biblical principles.

A fellow congressman objected, and pointed out that the government clearly based its policies on St Luke chapter two, verse 1.

Not knowing the text, the congressman sat down and withdrew his objection.

When he got home he checked the verse in his Bible.

'There went out a decree from Caesar Augustus that all the world should be taxed.'

Property

An elderly lecher with wandering hands was being shown round a house for rent by a pretty young estate agent.

'And are you to be let with the house, my dear?' asked the roué with a leer.

'No, I'm to be let alone,' replied the woman.

A surveyor appeared in court as an expert witness in a construction malpractice case.

After he was sworn in, the prosecuting barrister approached the man and said:

'Your name is Bernard Smith Frix?'

'No it is not,' replied the man.

Slightly discomposed, the barrister looked at his notes then looked at the man again.

'Bernard Smith Frix is the name on this paper. I repeat, this is your name.'

'And I repeat, it is not,' said the surveyor.

The barrister became red in the face and, grasping the lapels of his gown, pulled himself up to his full height.

'Please remember that you are under oath. I put it to you, that your name is Bernard Smith Frix.'

'And I put it to you that it is not,' replied the surveyor. 'My name is Bernard Smith, FRICS.'

Restaurants

A man took his fiancée to a fancy French restaurant that had just opened in London.

Hoping to impress his fiancée, the man tried out his schoolboy French with the waiter.

'Je...er...je vous...plait...le...quelque chose...'

'I'm sorry sir, I don't speak French' replied the waiter.

'Well dammit man, find someone who can!' snapped the man.

'A contented mind is a continual feast' as the old proverb says. That may be true, but a continual feast is the best way to get a contented mind.

'Have you prepared the oysters for dinner?' asked the restaurateur of the new cook.

'Yes sir,' said the chef. 'I've got them nice and clean and thrown away all the nasty stuff inside 'em.'

The Victorian artist Phil May, when once down on his luck in Australia, took a job as waiter in a very low-class restaurant. An acquaintance came into the place to dine, and was aghast when he discovered the artist was his waiter.

'My God!' he whispered. 'To find you in such a place as this.'

May smiled, as he retorted: 'Oh, but, you see, I don't eat here.'

An old New York toast: 'Here's champagne to your real friends, and real pain to your sham friends.'

Retirement

The CEO finally retired after forty years' service.

He spoke to his wife.

'Every morning you will wake me at five and say "time to go to the office, dear".

'Yes dear,' replied his wife.

'...and I shall turn over and say "damn the office" and go to sleep again', added the man.

'Today we would like to thank our boss Mr Jones for his service to our company. Mr Jones is someone who does not know the meaning of the word "impossible", who does not know the meaning of "lunch break", who does not understand the meaning of the word "no". So we have organised a whip round and bought him a dictionary.'

Wife: What are you doing today?

Retired husband: Nothing.

Wife: You did that yesterday.

Retired husband: I haven't finished it yet.

Scotsmen

A Scots businessman heard that Jews were very astute in business, and decided he would find out their secret. He visited the local rabbi and asked how the Jews became so wise.

The rabbi smiled and said 'We eat a certain kind of fish.'

'Oh aye, brain food!' cried the Scotsman. 'And if I eat some, will I be wise too?' asked the Scotsman.

'Maybe so, who can tell?' said the rabbi.

'How can I get some of this special fish?' said the Scotsman, excitedly.

The rabbi shrugged. 'I could sell you some, but it costs twenty pounds.'

The Scotsman agreed, and the rabbi took a small jar from the kitchen. The Scotsman handed over the money and took the jar.

Then he looked at the label.

'This is just pickled herring!' said the Scotsman. 'That doesn't cost twenty pounds a jar!'

The rabbi replied with a twinkle in his eye, 'see, you're getting wise already!'

McTavish (checking out of a hotel): Has all my luggage been brought doon?

Hotel porter: Yes sir.

McTavish: Are you sure I've left no' left anything in the room?

Hotel porter: No sir, not a penny!

Two Scotsmen were going home from the races. Mc Tavish spied a thick roll of banknotes that someone had dropped on the ground. He picked it up excitedly and flicked through the notes.

McDougal sighed and looked on with admiration. 'My but you're a lucky fellow, McTavish,' he said.

'Huh!' exclaimed McTavish. 'Call that lucky – it's all fivers – not a single tenner among them!'

Tourist (to Scotsman): Does it always rain here?

Scotsman: No, it snows sometimes.

A Scots chemistry teacher was giving a demonstration to his pupils. He dropped a pound coin into a beaker of acid and asked:

'Now class, will this coin be dissolved by the acid?'

One pupil put his hand up. 'No sir, it definitely will not!'

The teacher smiled. 'That's right, lad - well done! Now, can you explain why?'

The boy smiled back, 'Well, if the acid was going to dissolve your coin, you would have used a penny.'

Two Scotsmen were discussing their dating experiences.

'Mon,' said McNab, 'if ye've taken a lassie oot for a fish supper, a visit to the pictures and given her a taxi ride home, can ye not give her a wee kiss goodnight?'

'Certainly not,' replied McTavish. 'Sounds like ye've done enough fae her already!'

Two Scottish expatriates in the Far East were discussing how they kept cool in the blazing tropical heat.

'I've got a folding fan,' boasted Mc Tavish, 'and I've used the same one for ten years. I just open a tiny bit of the fan when I use it, so as not to wear the rest oot.'

'Spendthrift!' replied Mc Dougal. 'I jist hold the fan still in front of my face and nod ma heid up and doon!'

In the Western Isles of Scotland a mother admonished her son for playing football in the front garden on a Sunday.

'Go and play football in the back garden out of sight,' she said. 'Do ye not know it's the Sabbath day?'

'Is it no' the Sabbath day in the back garden then?' asked the boy.

An Englishman was nodding off to sleep in a sleeping compartment on the London to Inverness train.

At Derby a Scotsman got on the train and was shown into the compartment by the guard.

The Scotsman noticed the Englishman's washbag by the sink. Thinking the Englishman asleep, the Scotsman took out the Englishman's toothbrush and brushed his teeth with it.

The Englishman had noticed, however, and determined to get even.

The next morning as the train passed through the Highlands, the Scotsman awoke to find the Englishman vigorously cleaning the soles of his shoes with the toothbrush.

'Whisht, whit are ye using yon wee brush for like that!' wailed the Scot.

'Oh, I always use this old toothbrush for this,' said the Englishman with a smile.

Shopping

The shop girl was fed up with the rude old woman trying to buy a broom.

'This one's too short,' moaned the woman. 'I'll hurt my back using it. Do you want me to cripple myself?' she said of one item she was shown.

The girl showed her another. 'Call this good quality?' asked the woman angrily. 'The handle will break the moment I use it. Typical of your company's standards.'

Eventually the woman reluctantly chose a broom. 'It's the shoddiest thing I've seen but it will have to do,' she said.

'Would madam like me to wrap it,' said the shopgirl, '...or would madam prefer to ride it home?'

A well known supermarket chain is selling a new miracle slimming bread. It is so light that a pound loaf only weighs eight ounces.

A middle aged bachelor put his small basket of goods on the supermarket checkout. The pretty young girl on the till looked at his items as she scanned them, then looked at the man.

'You're single, aren't you?' she asked.

'How did you know?' exclaimed the man in surprise. 'Could you tell that just by looking at the things I'm buying?'

The girl looked him up and down.

'No, because you're ugly.'

A woman visited an antiques shop and spoke to the owner.

'When I was in here last week I saw a big mug with an ugly face and a flat head, that held a lot of beer. I'd like to buy it.'

'Sorry,' replied the owner, 'but I can't possibly sell you that.'

'Oh, what a pity, but why not?' enquired the woman.

'That's my husband.'

A vacuum cleaner salesman knocked on the door of a run-down council house. A woman in curlers and a dressing gown, with a cigarette dangling from her mouth, answered the door.

'Good morning, madam,' said the salesman brightly, brandishing one of his products. 'I represent the Bettaclean Vacuum Cleaner Company.'

He then proceeded to open a bag and empty a large pile of dust and dirt on the hall carpet.

'If this vacuum cleaner can't clean that mess up, I'll eat it.'

The woman shuffled into the kitchen, came back and handed the man a wooden spoon.

'You'd better get started then. We've had our electric cut off.'

An eighteenth century bishop is said to have remarked to his clerical tailor, 'how is it you have not called upon me for your bill?'

'Oh,' said the tailor, 'I never ask a gentleman for money.'

'Indeed!' said the prelate, 'then what do you do if he doesn't pay?'

'Well,' replied the tailor, 'after a certain time I conclude that he is not a gentleman, and then I ask him.'

The owner of an antiques shop was proudly showing a group of tourists a rusty old horseshoe priced at two thousand pounds.

'This is the shoe of the horse ridden by Richard the Third at the Battle of Bosworth.'

The tourists murmured in appreciation, until the tour guide stepped forward and spoke.

'I thought Richard the Third didn't have a horse. That's why he said "my kingdom for a horse."'

The shop keeper paused for a moment.

'Exactly. This is the shoe of the horse he didn't have.'

'You'll never catch a lie coming out of my mouth,' boasted the used car dealer.

'They come out so fast it would be impossible,' observed a customer.

Teachers

Teacher: in which of his battles was King Harold killed?

Pupil: I'm pretty sure it was the last one.

Teacher: Your new textbooks cost the school a fortune. Make sure you don't ruin them.

Pupil: You can trust me, sir. I won't lay a finger on them!

A pretty young blonde was taking her first driving lesson.

'Would you like to see where I was vaccinated?' she asked the instructor.

'Oh yes!' replied the man, eagerly.

'Over there, in that hospital,' replied the blonde.

Religious Education teacher: Who was sorry when the Prodigal Son returned?

Little Johnny: The fatted calf?

Teacher: Johnny, what is the difference between ignorance and indifference?

Little Johnny: I don't know and I don't care.

Travel

Two Americans were boasting of their distinguished family trees.

'My ancestors came over in the Mayflower' said one.

'Really?' said the other. 'Mine had their own boat.'

EuroHeaven: a place where the police are British, the cooks are French, the mechanics are German, the lovers are Italian and the management is Swiss.

EuroHell: a place where the police are German, the cooks are English, the mechanics are French, the lovers are Swiss and the management is Italian.

Undertakers

With great trepidation, the young policeman pulled back the sheet from the face of the corpse in the mortuary.

The elderly man with him looked down at the body and began crying and wailing.

'You and your wife must have been very close,' said the constable, patting the man on the shoulder in an attempt to console him.

'We hated each other!' wailed the man.

'Then why are you crying?' asked the officer in confusion.

'Because that's not her!'

With great sensitivity the undertaker asked Jones if he would like his late mother-in-law cremated or buried. 'Let's not take any chances,' said Jones. 'Do both.'

An undertaker was complaining of a falling off in trade.

'I haven't buried a living soul in weeks,' he said.

A man jumped into a stationary taxi. He wasn't sure if the driver had seen him so he leant forward and tapped him on his shoulder. The driver leapt out of his seat and clutched at his heart, turning round to look behind him with an expression of horror.

'What on earth's the matter?' asked the passenger.

'I'm sorry sir,' said the driver. 'You just gave me a bit of a shock. This is only my first day driving a taxi. Before that I drove a hearse!'

'I'm interested in the budget funeral plan.'

'Certainly sir, that'll be £49.99.'

'That's amazingly good value, I'll take it.'

'Would you like any extras, sir?'

'Such as what?'

'Such as a coffin?'

A man's wife died suddenly. As the pallbearers carried her coffin through the churchyard, one of them caught his foot on a tree stump and fell. The coffin crashed to the ground and the husband was astonished to see his wife climb out, having miraculously recovered.

She lived another ten years. When she finally died, the cortege was passing through the churchyard once more.

'For God's sake watch out for the stump!' shouted the husband.

Writers and artists

The celebrated writer Dr. Johnson was once asked by an aspiring novelist to give his opinion of a new work she had just written; adding, that if it did not interest him he should say so, for she had other 'irons in the fire', and if it was not likely to succeed, she could bring out something else.

'Then,' said the Doctor, after having turned over a few pages, 'I advise you, Madam, to put it where your other irons are.'

Artist Pablo Picasso surprised a burglar at work in his new chateau. The intruder got away, but Picasso told the police he could do a rough sketch of what he looked like. On the basis of his drawing, the police arrested a mother superior, the minister of finance, a washing machine, and the Eiffel Tower.

The dancer Isadora Duncan once wrote to George Bernard Shaw declaring that, given the principles of eugenics, they should have a child together.

'Think of it!' she enthused. 'With my body and your brains, what a wonder it would be.'

'Yes,' Shaw replied. 'But what if it had my body and your brains?'

Definition of a modern artist: someone who paints on a canvas, wipes it off with a cloth, and sells the cloth.

One day during a lecture tour, Mark Twain entered a local barber shop for a shave. This, Twain told the barber, was his first visit to the town.

'You've chosen a good time to come,' he declared.

'Oh?' Twain replied.

'Mark Twain is going to lecture here tonight. You'll want to go, I suppose?'

'I guess so...'

'Have you bought your ticket yet?'

'No, not yet.'

'Well, it's sold out, so you'll have to stand.'

'Just my luck,' said Twain with a sigh. 'I always have to stand when that fellow lectures!'

A story is told of the Victorian painter J.M.W Turner, who was once asked by a Scotsman in a railway carriage what he did for a living.

'I'm a painter,' replied Turner.

'Is that so?' said the Scotsman. 'If ye're wanting a few gallons of paint, I know where I can get you some for a guid price.'

'That's very kind of you,' replied the artist, 'but I only use a few ounces or so a year.'

The Scotsman shook his head, sighed and said 'Aye, business is pretty bad everywhere these days.'

Other titles from Montpelier Publishing

Humour and puzzles

The Book of Church Jokes

After Dinner Laughs

Scottish Jokes

Welsh Jokes

The Bumper Book of Riddles, Puzzles and Rhymes

Wedding Jokes

A Little Book of Limericks

The Father Christmas Joke Book for Kids

Men's interest

The Pipe Smoker's Companion

Advice to Gentlemen

The Frugal Gentleman

The Men's Guide to Frugal Grooming

The Real Ale Companion

The Cigar Collection

Printed in Great Britain
by Amazon

33972948R00036